THIS, PLEASE

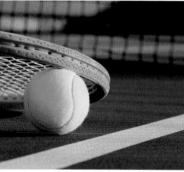

THIS, PLEASE

THE TOURIST
PICTURE
DICTIONARY

MICHAEL O'MARA BOOKS

First published in Great Britain in 2011 by
Michael O'Mara Books Limited
9 Lion Yard
Tremadoc Road
London SW4 7NQ

A CIP catalogue record for this book is available from the British Library.

Papers used by Michael O'Mara Books Limited are natural, recyclable products made from wood grown in sustainable forests. The manufacturing processes conform to the environmental regulations of the country of origin.

ISBN: 978-1-84317-573-5

1 2 3 4 5 6 7 8 9 10

www.mombooks.com

www.shutterstock.com

Cover design by Ana Bjezancevic

Designed and typeset by Design23

Printed and bound in Italy by L.E.G.O.

CONTENTS

Introduction

Need an extra bed in your hotel room? Can't remember the local word for lobster? In search of a plaster for a cut thumb? Whether you are on holiday or on a business trip, there are so many times when – no matter how hard you try to speak the language like a native – you find yourself in need of a word or phrase that you can't quite recall. Well, with this little gem of a book in your briefcase or backpack, your problems are over.

Broken down into six useful sections, and with a page highlighting food allergies in the food section and an 'information section' at the very back of the book that features all those things you may need in a hurry, all you have to do is flick to the page, find the image you're looking for, point to it and say, 'This, please!'

Simple!

The six sections each have their own distinctive icon for easy reference:

Transport – from planes, trains and buses to cars, bikes and motorcycles, all your transport requirements are found on these pages.

Accommodation – whether you're on business or backpacking, flick to these pages to make sure you get exactly what you want out of your accommodation.

Food – from breakfast, lunch and supper dishes to fast food and the most common food allergies, you can enjoy all the food you want to eat, wherever you are in the world.

Leisure – from sport to theatre, disco to the cinema, you'll find all the leisure activities you could wish for in these pages.

Shopping – from food items to shopping for clothes, accessories or mementoes, just point to what you need.

Medical & Information – whether you have cut your finger or need a dentist; need a mobile phone charger or a fire station, these useful images will get you out of any fix.

MÉTRO

Sleeper

BUS

HAIR
Conditioner
Shampoo

BATH
Gel

BODY
Lotion

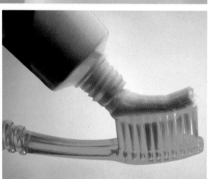

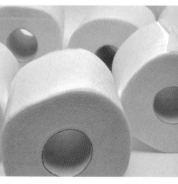

18

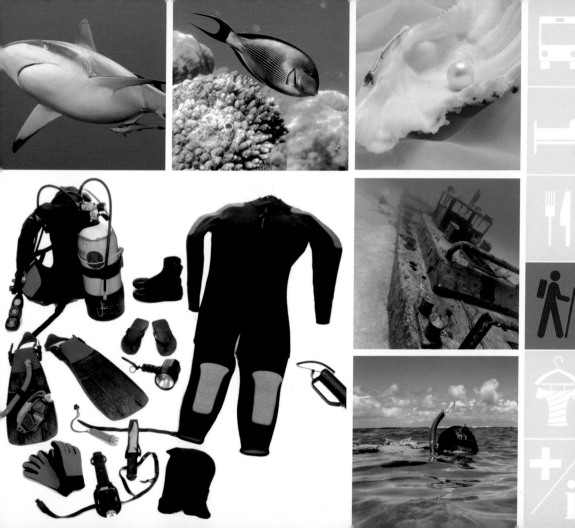

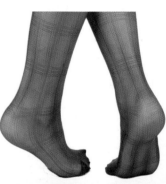

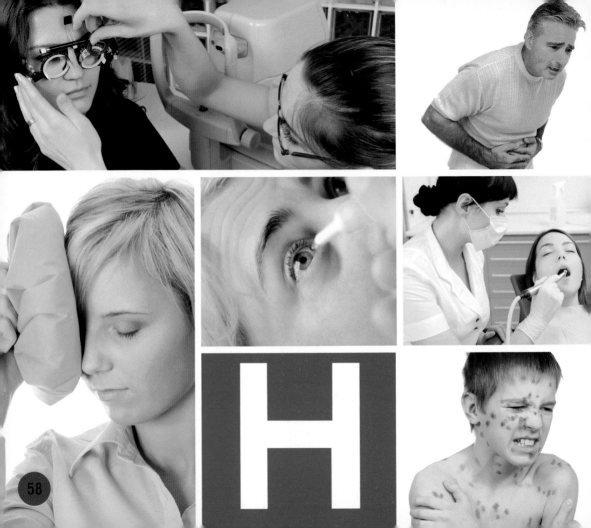

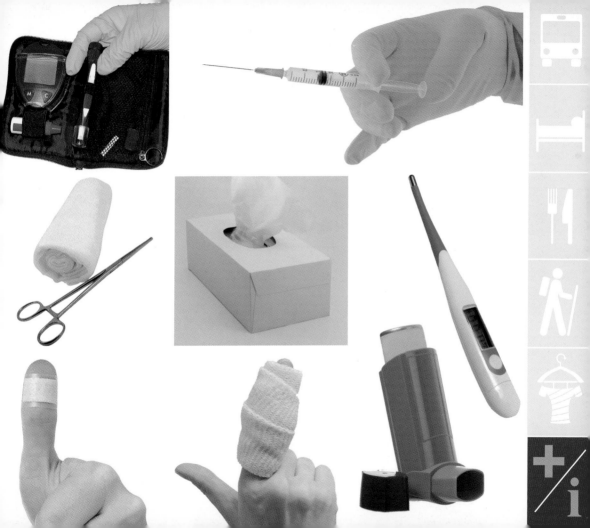

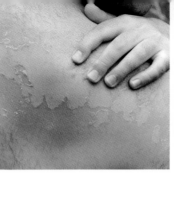

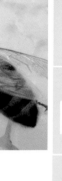

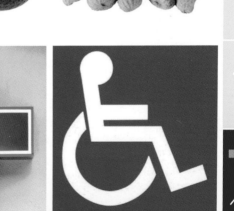

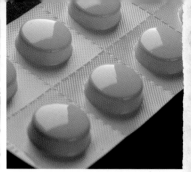